Demolition Derby

Jeff Savage

Illustrated with photographs
by Larry Buche

Capstone Press
MINNEAPOLIS

Printed in the United States of America.

Capstone Press • 2440 Fernbrook Lane • Minneapolis, MN 55447

Editorial Director   John Coughlan
Managing Editor   John Martin
Production Editor   James Stapleton
Copy Editor   Thomas Streissguth

Library of Congress Cataloging-in-Publication Data
Savage, Jeff, 1961--
    Demolition derby / Jeff Savage
      p. cm. -- (Motorsports)
    Includes bibliographical references and index.
    Summary: Includes a play-by-play account of a demolition derby, descriptions of different types of vehicles used, explanations of various kinds of derbies, and a glossary of terms.
    ISBN 1-56065-259-4
    1. Demolition derbies--Juvenile literature. 2. Automobile racing--Juvenile literature. [1. Demolition derbies. 2. Automobile racing. 3. Automobiles, Racing.]   I. Title. II. Series.
    GV1029.S19   1996
    796.7'2--dc20   95-7188
                                                CIP
                                                AC

Table of Contents

Chapter 1

A Great Demolition Derby

The crowd filed into Olympic Stadium in Montreal, Quebec, Canada. More than 54,000 fans had come to watch the two-day demolition derby.

Three friends–Luc Garand, Claude Lefebure, and Francois Levasseur–met in the pit area to register their pickup trucks. Luc had won the derby in Montreal the year before. This time, he would drive an orange Chevy truck. Claude would drive a yellow

This pickup has already been around the track a few times. The steel brace on its door helps the driver stay in the race.

Chevy pickup. Francois would drive a white Ford pickup with cartoon characters painted on its sides.

Off and Running

The pickups were ready. The signaler waved a green flag to start the competition.

The trucks moved in all directions. They dodged around the stadium floor, zigzagging every which way. Suddenly one truck crashed into another. *Wham!* Then two others smashed into each other. *Slam!* The crowd screamed with delight.

A pickup crunched Luc's orange truck from the side. Another whacked Claude's yellow pickup from behind. Two trucks hit Francois's white Ford pickup at the same time.

One truck conked out. Then another broke down. Francois's truck was the next to go. When Claude's truck overheated, he was out, too.

Two Trucks Left

Soon, only two trucks were left–Luc's orange Chevy and a blue Ford pickup. The two pickups dashed and darted across the stadium's dirt field. They swerved past one another, missing a hard collision by only a few inches. Then the blue Ford drilled the back of Luc's truck. His orange pickup coughed and sputtered and finally gave out.

Luc Gives Up His Truck

Because other drivers had damaged Claude's yellow truck so badly, he would not be able to compete the next night. Luc came to the rescue. He let Claude take any parts from his truck that Claude might need to fix his own.

Claude replaced his transmission and **running gear** with equipment from Luc's truck. Francois helped. Together they worked most of the night. By the following afternoon, Claude's yellow pickup was working again.

The Second Night

Claude and Francois returned to the **pit area** for the second night of racing. Soon the derby began. Trucks crissed and crossed and charged. *Wham! Crack! Crunch!* The pickups slammed into one another with terrific force. Eventually, there were just two drivers left–Claude and Francois.

Two Friends Square Off

Claude took aim at Francois's white truck and plowed toward it. Francois closed his eyes,

A good demolition derby leaves pickup trucks in bad shape.

clenched his teeth, and held the steering wheel. *Wham!* Claude slammed into the front of Francois's pickup.

Francois turned the ignition key. But Claude had damaged his truck too much, and it wouldn't start. He signaled to Claude that he was finished. Claude had won the derby.

Chapter 2
Not Like Other Motorsports

In most motorsports, drivers try to avoid crashing. This is not so in demolition derbies. It is the only motorsport in which drivers smash into the other vehicles on purpose. The last vehicle left running is the winner.

How the sport began is a mystery. Whatever their origin, demolition derbies are now popular everywhere in North America. Sponsors organize demolition events at county fairs and tracks, arenas, and stadiums throughout the United States and Canada.

Derbies feature different types of vehicles. The competitors use cars, trucks, jeeps, tractors or big-rig semitrailer trucks. Vehicles of the same kind always compete against each other. Pickups, for example, always battle pickups. And semis always battle semis.

Registration

To compete in a demolition derby, drivers register their vehicles and pay a pit fee. A derby official then inspects the vehicles. This inspection is called "teching." The official makes sure the vehicles have certain mechanical and safety features.

The Rules

For demolition-derby racing, the rules are simple. Drivers must crash into another vehicle at least once every minute. Crashing head-on is not allowed, and drivers cannot smash into the driver's side door. Drivers are not allowed to drive in a wild and uncontrolled way. Vehicles cannot leave the **boundary area**.

Drivers jockey for position in a hard-fought derby.

Nor can a driver leave his vehicle during a derby unless it catches fire.

How It Works

Demolition derbies are simple contests. Drivers bash their vehicles together until all but one of the vehicles are knocked out of competition.

Even with a bent wheel, you can stay in the derby.

A vehicle is out of a race when its driver cannot restart the motor within two minutes. A vehicle is also eliminated if it does not make contact with another vehicle every minute; if it leaves the boundary area; or if one of its tires is knocked completely off its rim.

Indoor derbies often have a time limit, usually 30 minutes. If two or more cars are running when the derby ends, a winner is determined by crowd response. The driver that gets the loudest applause when he or she steps out of the vehicle is the winner.

Derby Officials

Two signalers stand just outside the boundary area at a demolition derby. They wave a green flag to signal the start of the race. If a car catches fire or rolls over, the signalers use a red flag to signal a time-out. A checkered flag declares the winner.

Other officials watch the competition from the pit area. There is usually one official for every vehicle. These officials use a stopwatch to time the hits by vehicles. If a vehicle goes more than a minute without making a hit, an official alerts the signalers, who will eliminate that vehicle. Officials also eliminate drivers for being too reckless.

Chapter 3

The History of Demolition Derbies

The origin of demolition-derby racing is not known. But one man is credited with popularizing the motorsport. His name is Larry Mendelsohn. In 1957, Mendelsohn raced a stock car at Islip Speedway in New York. He lost control and crashed into the bleachers. Larry was fine, but his car was a wreck.

Spectators gathered around the smashed car. Mendelsohn was amazed at their reaction to his banged-up vehicle. Seeing an opportunity, he borrowed $1,000 from friends and began putting on shows of crashing cars.

ABC-TV's "Wide World of Sports" televised the world demolition derby championships at Islip Speedway. Viewers loved the event.

The Greatest Demolition Derby Ever

The greatest demolition derby in history took place in 1973 at the Los Angeles Memorial Coliseum. It was a smashup worth $100,000 in prize money. The sponsors billed the event as the World's Richest Demolition Derby. More than 50,000 people came to see the best derby drivers in North America.

But that was not all. Some of the greatest auto racers in the world competed. Among them were Parnelli Jones, Mario Andretti, and brothers Bobby and Al Unser. These racers knew Indy car racing and stock-car racing. They didn't realize that derby driving requires skill and technique, but they soon found out. Bobby Unser's Rolls Royce was knocked out of the derby in the first minute. Experienced derby drivers eliminated the other auto racers soon after.

Eventually, the derby came down to two cars–a 1973 Ford LTD, which Ken McCain drove, and a 1970 Mercury station wagon, driven by Tom Zumwalt. The two cars whacked each other so many times that they were both crippled. Finally, McCain stomped on the **accelerator** pedal. His black LTD charged at Zumwalt's car. *Blam!* He knocked it out. The signalers waved the checkered flag, and McCain was the winner.

After the derby, workers stacked the demolished cars in a heap. Then daredevil Evel Knievel jumped over them on his motorcycle in a spectacular leap.

Today's Derbies

Demolition-derby racing has not changed much in 20 years. The vehicles are safer, with better reinforced bracing and **fire-retardant** materials. But there have not been great technical changes in the vehicles. This is because derbies do not permit it. Drivers cannot **turbocharge** their engines. Also, they cannot alter their tires.

Chapter 4

The Vehicles

Most motorsports feature ultra-modified vehicles with high-performance engines. This is not so in demolition-derby racing. The idea is to wreck the vehicle. Fitting a derby vehicle with expensive gadgets would be like pouring money down the drain.

Drivers often get their derby cars from the junk heap. When drivers choose derby vehicles, they stick to the principle that bigger is better. Derby officials usually set no weight limit for vehicles. The only requirement is that

A little engine smoke won't stop a skilled demolition driver.

a vehicle cannot be fitted with parts from another kind of vehicle. For example, drivers cannot use truck parts to make their cars stronger or bigger. They can only use parts from other cars.

Favorite Cars

The demolition-derby cars drivers like best are **full-frame** cars. These cars are built on a full box frame made of heavy-gauge steel. The body and the frame are separate pieces. (Most cars built today have unibody construction. In these cars, the body and frame are one piece.)

Full-frame cars generally weigh about 5,000 pounds (2,268 kilograms). Unibody cars weigh as little as half that.

Car makers built these sturdy full-frame cars in the 1960s and 1970s. Among the most durable are:

1) Chrysler Imperials, Newports, and New Yorkers
2) Chevrolet Impalas, Caprices, and Monte Carlos
3) Ford LTD Wagons
4) Buick Electras and Oldsmobiles.

Chrysler Imperials are so rugged, in fact, that many derbies do not allow them.

Some drivers find that cars of unibody construction can be smashed more easily. Chevrolet Camaros, Pontiac Firebirds, and Ford Mustangs are examples of unibody vehicles.

Favorite Trucks

When it comes to demolition-derby trucks, the bigger they are, the better they are. Chevrolet trucks seem to be the most popular. Ford and Dodge pickups are favorites, too. Smaller, imported trucks hardly stand a chance in a derby.

Preparing the Vehicle

Drivers **strip** their vehicles before the contest. They remove hubcaps and horns. They replace the regular fuel tank with a smaller tank that they strap down behind the driver's seat. They usually remove all the glass, including the windshield, windows, and headlights.

Drivers chain down the front hood so it doesn't fly up during the derby. They cut a

Bent out of shape, a Chevy pickup circles for another run at the opposition.

basketball-sized hole in the hood so they can get to the engine easily in case of fire. They weld metal tow eyelets to the front and back of the vehicle so that a tow truck can remove it quickly from the track.

Full-size, U.S.-made pickups are tough competitors. Imports don't have a chance against them.

Drivers install a sturdy **roll bar** (usually a steel pipe) in their vehicles. They wrap longacre padding around the bar. Sometimes, they will also bolt channel steel along the sides of their cars. This is the only bracing derby officials permit.

Engines

A derby vehicle does not need a powerful engine. Many drivers replace the stock engine with a smaller one that allows for more room between the radiator and the engine's fan. This offers protection to the engine cooling system.

Tires

Demolition derbies allow only stock tires. They usually permit mud and snow tires. No brand of tire is preferred. Drivers often say that "the best tires are free tires."

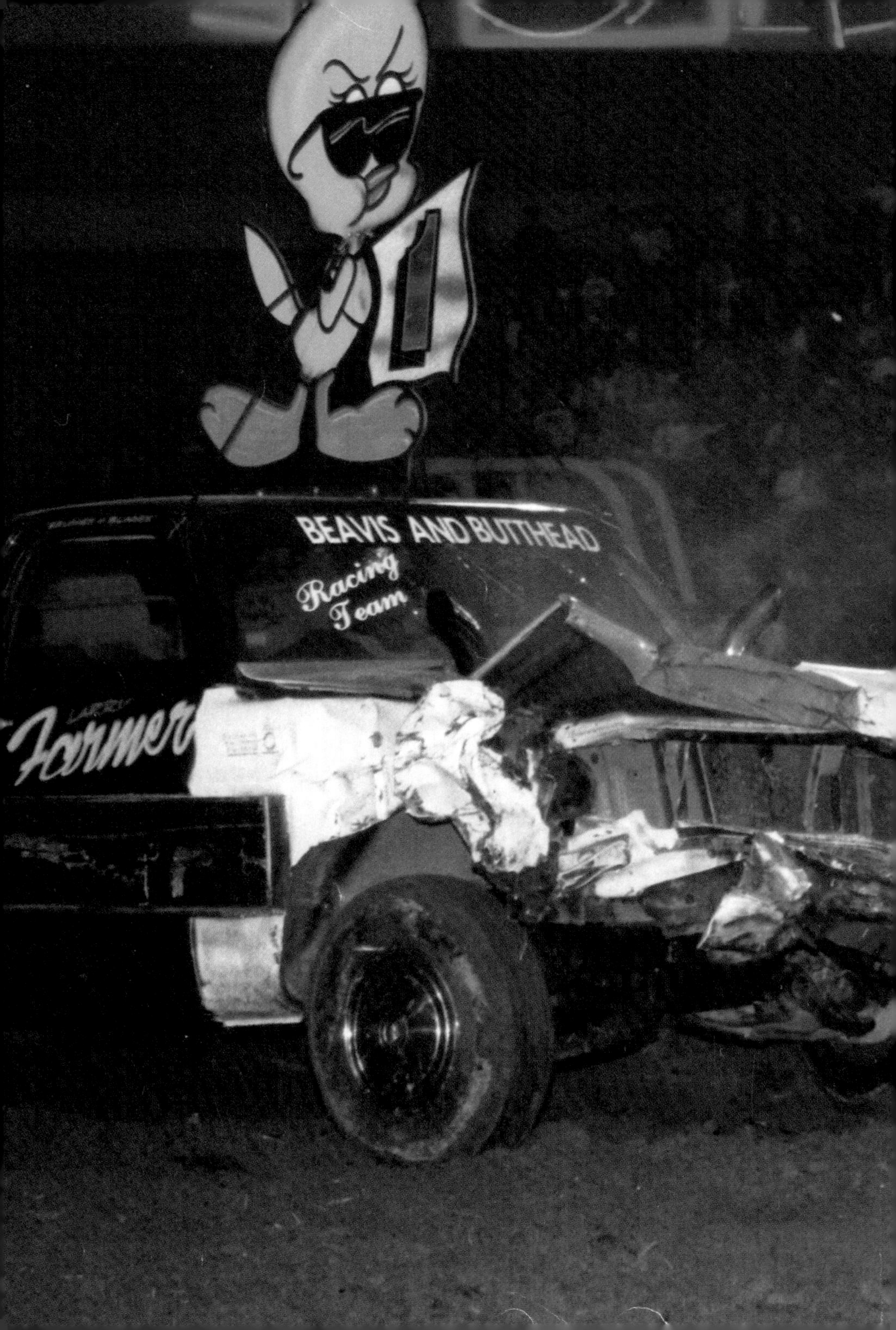

BEAVIS AND BUTTHEAD
Racing Team
Farmer

Chapter 5

Kinds of Demolition Derbies

Demolition derbies are not all the same. There are different kinds of tracks and several track configurations. There are also many kinds of races.

Track surfaces can be cement, dirt, or mud. The most common track shapes are ring, oval, and figure-8.

The Ring-Track Derby

The **ring-track derby** is the standard demolition derby. In this kind of derby

Ring-track derbies are free-for-alls, where drivers can maneuver anywhere within a large circle.

vehicles can go anywhere within a large circle. A vehicle is disqualified for leaving the circle.

The Oval-Track Derby

In the **oval-track derby,** the vehicles crash into one another while driving around an oval-shaped track. The winner is the last vehicle left running.

The Figure-8 Derby

The **figure-8** derby is like the oval derby. But in this event, vehicles drive on a track shaped like the number "8." The vehicles cross and crash into one another at the track's middle point. Drivers call this point the "X."

The Headlight Derby

Headlights are usually removed from demolition derby vehicles. In a headlight

The smoke and steam of overheated engines and busted radiators make a thick fog over the track.

derby, however, headlights are left in the cars. The stadium lights are turned off. The last car running with a headlight still working is the winner.

The Balloon-Race Derby

In this derby, a balloon is attached to the front and back of each car. When both balloons have been popped, officials eliminate the car from the competition.

The Backward Derby

Vehicles in this derby are allowed to drive backward only.

The Sack Derby

This derby calls for two people in each car. The driver wears a sack over his head. A teammate in the passenger's seat gives directions to the driver.

The Cat-and-Mouse Derby

This kind of derby is limited to 10 cars. Nine cars, called "cat cars," chase a single "mouse car" around the track. The mouse car wins if it can go around the track five times without getting knocked out.

The Football Derby

Two teams compete against each other in this kind of derby. Each team is made up of four American-made cars. They fight to push a little imported car over the other's goal line.

Chapter 6

Drivers and Strategies

Most derby drivers are not professionals. The sport does not offer enough prize money for drivers to make a living at it.

Drivers might be truck drivers or shop owners or mechanics or plumbers. They compete strictly for the fun of fixing up a junker car and slamming it into other junker cars.

Demolition-derby drivers do not compete in **circuits.** There is little sponsorship money because vehicles do not use the latest gadgets or promote the newest products. And the prize money is small compared to other motorsport competitions. When they win, drivers usually use their prize money to fix up their next junker car.

By the end of the race, good cars have turned into worthless piles of junk.

Most derby participants are men. But some women compete as well. Drivers often compete in their first derby as soon as they get their driver's license. Most drivers quit before age 50.

Tricks to Improve Vehicles

Smart drivers often try to improve their vehicles' durability. They will remove the cooling fan to create more space under the hood. They may move the battery to the front seat, pack the engine block with oatmeal, or sprinkle black pepper to slow water seepage.

Drivers use many tricks like these. As long as the tricks are within the rules, they're a legal part of demolition-derby racing–no matter how strange they may seem.

Sponsors have turned this car into a demolition-derby billboard.

Chapter 7
Safety

Derby officials do everything possible to ensure the safety of the drivers. After all, safety is always more important than winning.

Drivers wear helmets to protect their heads. These helmets are made of a hard plastic material called **Kevlar**. They are more solid than football helmets.

Derby vehicles often catch fire. A fireproof sheet of metal between the engine and the driver serves as protection. Drivers wear fireproof suits made of flame-retardant cotton material. Also, all vehicles have a fire extinguisher in the cab.

Drivers wear a seat belt and a **shoulder harness**. The seat belt goes across the driver's lap. The shoulder harness extends across the driver's chest from shoulder to lap.**Injuries**

Even though drivers are well-protected, they still get injured.

A driver at the Maricopa County Fairgrounds in Phoenix, Arizona, suffered a broken leg when a car rammed through his door. At a derby in Roseville, California, one car slammed another so hard it knocked the driver into the trunk. At Spanaway Speedway in Washington, a crash knocked a driver unconscious. When he came to, he found himself sitting in the stands with people he did not know. In a derby at the Missouri State Fair in Sedalia, a car struck a Chevrolet Estate Wagon so hard that it flew into the air and landed on top of another car.

A medical crew and a fire crew are present at every race. Two licensed emergency medical technicians stand by with an ambulance. The fire crew consists of four officials. They operate the fire extinguishers and hoses hooked to water hydrants.

Glossary

accelerator–the foot pedal that controls the amount of fuel passed from the tank to the cylinder

boundary area–the area in which derby vehicles must remain or be disqualified

circuit–a series of events in which points are awarded

figure-8 derby–a derby in which vehicles crash while racing around a track shaped like the number "8"

fire-retardant–slow to catch fire

flagman–the person who uses flags to signal the beginning and end of a derby

full-frame–having a full box frame or chassis made of heavy-gauge steel

Kevlar–a hard plastic material used to make the helmets worn by demolition-derby drivers

oval-track derby–a derby in which vehicles crash while racing around an oval-shaped track

pit area–the area near the track where the drivers prepare their vehicles for the derby

ring-track derby–the standard derby, in which vehicles compete in a circle

roll bar–a protective bar (usually a steel pipe) above and around the driver that prevents the vehicle's roof from collapsing in a rollover

running gear–a moving part with grips (called "teeth") connected to the wheels. The two gears on a derby vehicle are forward and reverse.

shoulder harness–a protective belt that extends across a driver's chest from shoulder to lap

stripped–when the windshield, horn, and other items have been removed from a derby vehicle

turbocharged–made more powerful by the addition of a blower that gives the engine compressed air

To Learn More

Atkinson, E.J. *Monster Vehicles*. Mankato, MN: Capstone Press, 1991.

Holder, Bill and Harry Dunn. *Monster Wheels*. New York: Sterling Publishing, 1990.

Johnson, Scott. *Monster Truck Racing*. Minneapolis: Capstone Press, 1994.

————. *The Original Monster Truck: Bigfoot*. Minneapolis: Capstone Press, 1994.

Savage, Jeff. *Monster Truck Wars*. Minneapolis: Capstone Press, 1995.

————. *Mud Racing*. Minneapolis: Capstone Press, 1995.

————. *Truck and Tractor Pulling*. Minneapolis: Capstone Press, 1995.

Sullivan, George. *Here Come the Monster Trucks*. New York: Cobblehill Books, 1989.

Some Useful Addresses

Monster Truck Racing Association
6311 N Lindbergh Boulevard
Hazelwood, MO 63042

SRO Motorsports
477 E Butterfield Road
Suite 400
Lombard, IL 60148

USA Motorsports
2310 West 75th Street
Prairie Village, KS 66208

National Hot Rod Association (NHRA)
2035 Financial Way
Glendora, CA 91740

Index